NOT

BEAUTIFUL
When Being Beautiful Is A Curse

Natalie M. Stewart

URBAN WORLD
PRESS

ISBN: 978-0-692-64151-4

Contents

Introduction

Not understanding at five years old, why were there such large fingers in my bed? My tiny fingers wrestling furiously with the large hand in my bed as tears ran down my face. My mind was puzzled with questions. *"Why was this hand larger than mine trying so hard to touch my innocent body?"* *"Why didn't the tears, and the look on my face not scare the man with the large hands?"* The last question was, *"why was he fighting so hard to touch me?"*

Hello, I am a woman that all her life was told how *"beautiful"* I was. Trying to yet understand why in my heart, mind, body, and soul did not feel so pretty and so *"NOT BEAUTIFUL."*

A baby girl was born to a mother that had the strength of a giant and a father whose identity at the time was not so clear, but as a child, I was told he was a *"BAD MOTHERFUCKER,"* according to the stories told by my family as a young girl. Two people that should not have at all procreated, brought into this cruel world a baby girl that would eventually become a grown woman with an identity crisis, confused about who her family was, and live a life full of lies, secrets, hurt, and deceit. On my birth certificate, it read my Dad was a concrete finisher and my Mother a Homemaker. Even my birth certificate was a lie. The lies continued from the birth of me until now.

CHAPTER 1
Isn't She Lovely

Unto us, a child is born. A bastard girl was given. This girl was hand picked by God to live a life of pain and strife. I had so many questions about myself that my head was on the verge of exploding. A mother who loved me so dearly, but at her being at almost 40 years of age, *"Why did she keep me and had no hand in the upbringing of my other siblings? What made me so beautiful to her that she felt I would add value to her own life? Why was I so special? Why was I her experiment in Child Upbringing 101?"* I remember as a child growing up, I was embraced with love from my entire family. Even though I had older siblings, three brothers, and one sister. I was raised as an only child because my oldest brother had already completed high school when I was born.

I was the apple of all three of my brother's eyes. I had a big sister and we were seven years apart. She was a doll that did all she could to protect me. I was like her little doll. She kept me well dressed and did her best even in her youth to save me from the same torture and pain she had suffered herself from some of the sick male bastards in our family. Yeah, it was a bunch of creepy sick motherfuckers in our family that adorned beautiful little girls.

Pedophiles and child molesters were hidden in this family and as children, the things they did to my sister and I began to be normal sick rituals. I had talked to as an adult, several women in the Tillman lineage. Yet back then women in our family were taught the *"Hush and Do Not*

Tell Policy." We kept all family issues within our family. *"A bunch of secrets of, pure mentally sick male motherfuckers, that has caused me to not once, not twice, but several times as an adult, to attempt to take my own life.*" The people in my family who I have told as of today have said, *"Hush it happened in all families you were just beautiful,"* so why am I in my mid 40's feeling, *"NOT SO BEAUTIFUL!"*

I came from a very large family. It was seven siblings in just my grandmother's generation. My family would always get together drinking and playing cards in my mother's home two houses down from my grandmother's house. All of the kids, some cousins and some friends of my family's kids were made to stay in the back room playing. I was the youngest, but I remember oh so well when my boy cousins would kiss me and touch me as a delicate flower. I felt that it was normal. I was a child, I did not know any better so I opened my legs and let my flower bloom for them to touch and pick away. Innocence stripped from me in a sick way. Being constantly told I was so lovely and so beautiful but in the right now, why am I feeling, *"NOT SO BEAUTIFUL?"*

Ashamed and so confused, I thought family was about love. Did I not deserve a normal childhood? I was taught to pray to the same God that the rest of my family prayed to. I felt he was not helping them evil no good bastards stay away from me, so why would God listen to the soul of a five-year-old broken little bastard girl? I had a hiding place though. Yeah! Didn't all little kids have one? Mine was two doors down at my grandmother's house. I hid and played under the two-plex coffee table by my Grandaddy's feet. My grandparents had a dog named Sherman, a full bred German Shepard that was very protective of me. That dog was my best friend and my playmate. Sherman and I would just talk as I rode down the alley at my grandparent's house.

My safe haven was at 2817 Central Avenue Gary, Indiana 46407. This place held a lot of safety and protection for a five-year-old little girl running from her own home just two doors down.

I really do not recall the address at the place I was supposed to call home, and *"I try my damnest to forget."* My grandparent's home was a safe haven full of love. I was actually happy there. The only happiness I remember as an adult. As a little girl, I could sit on Granddaddies lap laugh and be treated like the five-year-old princess I was. Plus my two brothers were there, my grandmother had raised them from birth. My brothers treated me like royalty. I felt *"SO BEAUTIFUL"* when I was there. My big brothers and my grandparents protected me. I was not old enough nor brave enough to tell them what was going on two doors down where I lived. Yet for some strange reason, I believe my grandmother sensed something was wrong. She loved me enough to look me in my eyes, but she knew that if I told her about the wild lifestyle two doors down with all the drinking, card playing and havoc, I was gonna get a good beating.

My sister and I were so afraid at home when parties went on. We would not come out of our room. I mean we were scared to go to the bathroom. We used a blue Tupperware cup that we peed in and would throw the pee out the window. To us it was normal. We had a love for our mom that was *"BIGGER,"* than all the water that ran through the earth, but she yearned the love from my Dad, Archie, Wilbur, and Roy.

Men were coming in the front door and flying out the back. My sister and I did not care. We loved our mother. We wanted our mother's love even though 44 years of my life I have yet to hear those three words from my mother

NOT BEAUTIFUL

"I LOVE YOU! PUZZLING!" I remember my mother as a beautiful, caramel woman that could, and would, steal the heart of any man. I am not sure, but I am willing to put money on this. I think men stole her heart quite a bit. I mean stolen and stepped on so much that "Schlitz Malt Liquor Bull," could not mend her heart. She held a lot in. No matter what we loved Mama. It's just at that time our love was not enough for her. She wanted so much more from love. She wanted the American dream. You know, *"a husband, a stable and solid home, great neighbors, well-educated children, and all the other good shit America has been lying about."* My poor enslaved mom did the best a mother could do or what she knew. I see now that she was chasing the wrong, *"LOVE."* Well this *"Apple of hers, (ME),"* did not fall far from the apple tree. Our track record speaks volumes. My Mom had five children with five different last names and myself. Well, I have four kids with four different last names, *"talk about generational curses."* Well, *"Got Dammit there you have it!"*

Chapter 2
On The Run

In my elementary life, me, my mom and my sister, lived the life of *"Forrest Gump without the millions."* We were *"running and running and running until Mama got tired."* Then eventually, we stopped *"IN PURE DE FUCKING HELL!"* I believe Modesto, California was what they called that dusty ass place. I called it *"NIGHTMARE ON FUCKING GREEN ACRES!"* Country as shit! My Mom had a cousin there with *"twelve motherfuckin kids,"* and as you know in all typical black families, they were scattered all over the damn family, but we kept it in the family with the rest of the lies and bullshit! *"UGH!"* I so hated that place.

As an adult, it holds a lot of painful memories. It had red dirt, chickens, a run through washer with a run through ringer that would chop your arms off if you missed a beat. We bathed in a big silver foot tub and shared the same nasty ass water with all the other children. It was slavery and we did chores like *"Kunta Kinte."* *"SHITTTT!"* So far away from Gary, Indiana, damn, I missed my grandparents. Then I had an aunt from country ass Winfield, Louisiana that could yell our names so damn loud we could hear her from California to Indiana. That shit got on my last nerves. My family in Indiana was smooth and laid back. My Grandmother would kill us dead if we reached that climax in our throat. Oh did I mention who my mom was running from. My gambling, drinking, two-timing daddy who even through his fucked up lifestyle, loved me to *"DEATH,"* but my Mama hated his damn guts. *"Lol!"* I can hear the *"Gap*

Band" now *singing, "YEARNING FOR YOUR LOVE."* I believe the hook was, *"You Can't Keep Running In and Out of My Life,"* and Daddy was notorious for that. My dad did what he damn well pleased. *"Lol!"* A *"5'ft. 5'-inch"* smoking pistol with the slickest grin a slickster could have. I inherited my dads slick grin. Nothing to brag on I also inherited his pot addiction. Daddy gave me my first joint and my first drink at fifteen years of age.

Out of my twelve cousins in Modesto, I had a favorite cousin beautiful, caramel, with light brown eyes. She had one girl and two boys. Her youngest son was my best bud. We were like *"two peas in a pod."* Like *"white on rice,"* we stuck together, yet he had an uncle who was also my cousin that was *"evil as hell and sick as shit!"* That bastard would volunteer to babysit us, or either our parents would leave us with his ass when they ran errands. He was passed sick. He was a perverted pedophile to the *"10th power."* Oh yeah, he was that ratchet. He did things so perverted to me and my little cousin that he may as well *"jacked off on a donkey and fucked him."* My cousin and I were two of the most beautiful *"big brown-eyed kids"* in the family, but that perverted son of a bitch made us feel so *"NOT BEAUTIFUL."*

As a little girl, it hurt me so bad because I felt I failed as a protector for my cousin, because as an innocent little boy, I saw fear in his big brown eyes. We were so afraid of this bastard that at night my cousin and I would make a protective tent. You know, like a shelter. We were so afraid we held each other at night. We were two young innocent kids and we would cry until we fell asleep. We were thankful that we did not get got in our sleep by this Pedophile aka, *"The Kid Creeper", aka "Dark Vader."* Two beautiful innocent kids innocence stripped away that made us both feel so *"NOT BEAUTIFUL."* Yet, as usual, my family had a "Hush no tell policy." Then once we became adults, I myself have been trying to figure out how this bastard was still alive and how we could get away with killing his ass.

Last I heard by some members of my family, this *"Motherfucker"* is still terrorizing kids in our family. I know of at least seven more young children in our family. *"I wonder what the statue of limitations are for getting this Jack Ass locked up or be put to a slow death."* I hope that when I finish writing this book that family member's would castrate this *"Fruity Kid Loving Motherfucker."* I am telling all! *"This hold back shit been going on too long."* Like *"Johnny Taylor"* said, *"Everything is out in the Open."* Me personally...I would like to hang him by his penis, pour gas on his ass and let the *"MOTHERFUCKER BURN!"* *"BURN, MOTHERFUCKER BURN!"* After all the therapy, counseling and psych meds, with this sucker still alive and running free, I deserve a bigger check from the state. One much bigger than the one I am getting today. I mean *"RAIGHT NAH!"*

My mom, my sister, part of the clan of twelve, and myself were forced to go to a church in Modesto. There was a Pastor at this church that they called Reverend Bassard. He was full of shit too. I was in the midst of some weird shit. It was more dysfunctional than a *"Pig fucking a chicken on the roof."* Those folks would be running, screaming, and vomiting up white stuff that was supposedly the devil. Them *"Negroes"* was the *"DEVIL!"* They called it the *"HOLY GHOST."* I saw the Ghost, but it was nothing Holy about this exorcist shit. The choir of three would be belting out this song called *"GOIN UP A YONDER."* My plea to God was let these fools go any damn where. I just wanted to get the hell out of this church immediately! If it took all this to go to heaven, I opted out and was positive I was a sure shot for *"HELL!"*

My grandmother would have never taken me to no shit like this three times a week and Sunday. In Gary, Indiana I was a proud member of New Mt. Moriah Missionary Baptist Church, real church. The *"Tom Foolery"* I had seen at Rev. Bassard's Church had to be hell. The streets of gold were the boards we could see through to cover the dirt bottom of that dusty ass church and the glorious clouds we seen came from the hole in the roof of the church. I begged the Lord do not let it rain, because if it did we were guaranteed a dirt bath. *"IT WAS NO WAY IN HELL,"* my grandmother would have put me in no shit like this and called it a *"HEAVENLY HOME."* This was nowhere near heavenly and fuck that home shit. My home was at 2817 Central Avenue with my grandmother. I did not want to be at this church. It was hell. They said Jesus was a carpenter. Well, Jesus needed a construction crew to blow that place up. To top it all off and prove the evil and spirit of death lurking around this place. One Sunday, we went to church and when the doors of the church flew open, Reverend Bassard's son had hung himself in the church. Yep, he killed himself. Says a lot about a dysfunctional church.

At that same church, my mom met this pastor by the name of Archie. He was a nice man. He was good to my mom, sister and I. He moved us from that house in Modesto to a house in the suburbs. We moved to Merced, California. Like the *"Jefferson's,"* we had moved on up. We had a big home, with a swimming pool in the back in an upscale neighborhood. We lived large, we lived good, but even *"THE DEVIL,"* knew the Bible. We really got to meet the real pastor, *"Reverend Satan Archie."* This man was the pastor and my mom was his First Lady. Well, until I seen the bastard first hand. His evilness lurked in the middle of the night.

My sister and I shared a room with twin beds. I pretended to be asleep. Then I watched this *"NO GOOD ASS PASTOR,"* climb in the bed with my sister. Yep! The life I thought we moved from in Modesto to Merced, California had come back to haunt us again. *"God, why?"* Our life was supposed to change. It was supposed to be made beautiful, but once again it was so *"NOT BEAUTIFUL!"* I mean, could my eyes be deceiving me? Could my sister and I just have been an attraction for pedophiles? I mean this *"Archie Cat was smooth as a Baby's Ass."* He had my poor mom fooled, but for some reason, far away in Gary, Indiana, yet again, my wise grandmother knew her granddaughters were not safe.

I will never forget my mom was frying chicken in the kitchen and Archie's slick ass playfully grabbed me as I was playing and running around the house. Archie then grabbed a blanket pretending he was covering me up and then the craziness began under that blanket. This bastard had the audacity to be playing with my nipples while my mama was in the kitchen frying chicken. *"WTF?"* This motherfucker had to be insane. If my mama would have known this bastard was doing this while frying chicken. His ass would have been a *"well-fried PREACHER!"* *"Fried, died, dead and kicked to the side."* He would have had a funeral right then. No preaching, just sad singing and fuck the flower bringing. A cremation would have been what they called it.

The nerve of this Nigga. What gave him the audacity to feel like he could lay his unholy hands on me? If my grandmother had known in detail what he was doing to us, she would have pumped his ass full of lead. *"Bye Mr. Preacher man!!!"* He would have really been *"holey!"* BANG BANG!!! Well, I don't know what my grandmother was feeling, but she was feeling some type of way. That old lady was on a plane leaving from Chicago to California. She came and got her daughter and her two granddaughters from a so-called, supposed to be *"beautiful life,"* that turned out to be so *"NOT BEAUTIFUL!"* That is why today a preacher can't tell me shit! God himself would have to say, *"Listen to this Nigga, he saying some good SHIT!"*

Chapter 3
Houston We Have A Problem

"WHO DA FUCK LIVE IN THIS COUNTRY MOTHERFUCKER?"
How in the cowboy hell did we get here? My mama told us her daddies people lived here...*"WTH?"* I thought my granddaddy was the man my grandmother was married to up in Gary, Indiana. Talking about a fucking identity crisis. Shit was not adding up and I was nine years old. It was some lies being told to me... *"OHHH WEEE MANN!"* I seen horses riding down the got damn street and at the time it wasn't no damn streets in this city. It was dirt roads with no lines. I guess if you crossed over you was a dead son of a bitch. *"OMG!"* When I met my so-called mama's family in Houston, I was like *"Sophia on Color Purple,"* but more graphic. *"HARPO WHO DA FUCK IS THESE PEOPLE?"* Mama, later on, had some series explaining to do. I was nine years old, but I knew my mama had fell and bumped her head. I didn't know these people and had never seen these folks in my life. *"TALKING ABOUT A SERIOUS IDENTITY CRISIS...I WAS FLABBERGASTED...Lord Ham Mercy!"*

I remember the sweetest old lady though that I could ever come across. Her name was Olivia, my mom's aunt. My so-called biological grandfather that I had not heard about until then was named Eddie Wilson. That explained why my mom's maiden name was Wilson and not Phipps. Phipps was the last name of the man I knew, as my grandfather that later on in my adulthood would find out was my dad's biological uncle. *"Uh...oh!"* Anyway, this old lady I was taught to call her Aunt Olivia, she was the epitome of *"LOVE."* She was, at that time, the backbone of my Houston-based family. She taught me that there was love in old Houston, Texas. I had family members on both sides of the street that were all very close. I felt a somewhat sense of family in Houston, but nothing like my grandmother's house. That was *"HOME!"*

As we settled in Houston I had an older brother that came here before us and got us an apartment in South Houston by a mall called "Gulfgate Mall." The apartments we lived in were called "Colonial Falls Apartments." It was Mom, my brother, his girlfriend, my sister and I. We were pretty safe there. My brother was in his early 20's and my sister was at the time about 15 years old. My big brother took great care of my sister and I. He was sort of like a dad, but better. He took such great care of us that his childish girlfriend was envious as hell. They fought like cats and dogs. My mom would try to stop them, but she was ignorant. He did not fight her but she fought him like a man. He had to sit on that fool until she fell asleep. My sister and I shared a room one door down from my brother and his then girlfriend. When she wasn't fighting with my brother she was sweet to my sister and me. At least, she pretended to be. She knew we were young so she would pick us for information and that led to more fights between her and my brother. *"That girl was some fries short of a damn Happy Meal!!!"*

We moved to Houston in the summertime. I had been in Gary, Indiana where it was all black. Well, the part where my family hung out and lived at. I was enrolled in a school in south Houston and I had never seen this race of such beautiful people in my life. They called them Mexicans. It was interesting, because when we moved to California and I briefly went to elementary school there, my best friends name was Kymeko and she was Japanese. At the time, that was what I was mainly surrounded by in Cali, Whites, and Orientals. Anyway, the Mexicans were cool kids. What I remember about that school was pleasant. They celebrated a holiday on May 5th called "Cinco De Mayo" and I enjoyed the food and the new language I was taught to speak, Spanish!

Mexicans were festive people that loved a good time. In the apartments we lived in, they loved beer and barbeque and my family hung with them as if we were one big family, finally, good times. There were blacks in my apartments as well. I will never forget I had a friend named Carmen. A pretty little black girl, but she was a bully. I remember her taking my then skates where I thought I was *"Kim Fields,"* you know *"Tootie"* from *"The Facts of Life."* Anyway, Carmen took my skates and I came to my apartment crying. My brother saw me crying and barefoot. I had never had a fight in my life then. My brother walked my barefoot ass back around that corner and told me to beat her ass or he was gonna kick mine. I have been kicking ass ever since. I was waxing her ass and my brother must have seen Mama coming. That sucker left me whipping Carmen's ass and I remember Mama grabbing me by the back of my shirt and she kicked my ass for fighting. I was damned if I did and damned if I didn't. Still wondering why my mama did not kick my brother's ass.

The whole apartment complex was family. My sister was excellent at braiding hair at 15 and at that time in the early 80's braids were the only way. We had started being friends with a family in the apartments by the last name called Hill. They had moved here from Timpson, Texas. I mean cool as shit. They had a *"biggggg"* family too. My sister made a lot of money braiding hair in that family. There was one brother in the family that was ten years older than my sister and he looked at her in a special way and she had a crush on this old man... *"OHHH I'M GONE TELL MAMA ON YOU!!!!"* This Cat had really befriended my mom. She thought he was the *"Messiah of the Ghetto."* Nice looking dark skin man, well-dressed, good job, greased her palm with cash every now and then and she saw him as a candidate for a son-in-law. *"So good that at 16 my sister had permission to date this Nigga."*

Well later on in Colonial Fall Apartments my brother and that crazy ass girlfriend stayed at it. I guess she was tired of not getting all his attention. One night when we were supposed to be sleeping. My sister and I heard a gunshot... *"POW POW"...* *"This bitch tried to kill my favorite brother in his sleep, but that Psycho Heifer missed the first time."* The bullet went straight through the wall in me and my sister's room. The next gunshot she was fucked. My brother then grabbed her and he should have beat her crazy ass, but he didn't. He subdued the gun, hog tied her ass, and put her on an airplane back to her mama. She was half Black and half Hawaiian. They say them mixed women are crazy and she was a lunatic. Years later he went back to that fool and had a baby. *"Where they do that shit at?"*

Now back to this *"ten years older Nigga"* that my sister loved. I could not believe this shit. I only had one sister and I was losing her to a complete stranger. I did not understand this old man younger woman shit. I was tired of all the bullshit. I missed my Grandmother in Gary, Indiana so much. The life in Houston that started out beautiful was so *"NOT BEAUTIFUL."* God had answered my prayers. Last I remember of Colonial Falls Apartments was me leaving and being put on an airplane to go spend the summer with my Grandmother in the *"GI!" "YES!"*

CHAPTER 4
LOVE AND REVELATION

There I was back in my loving Grandmothers arms. I had landed at O'Hare Airport in Chicago, Illinois. See even though we were from Gary, Indiana we had to fly into Chicago, which was 45 minutes from Gary. I missed that *"light-skinned, green-eyed stallion."* I must have hugged the life out of her. My grandmother could cook too. She had prepared a meal for a Queen and to top it off she added my favorite dessert. Her famous bread pudding. She was a beast in the kitchen. You could smell her bread pudding down the alley.

She taught me at ten years old how to roll dough for biscuits, cut teacakes, bake homemade pound cakes, and let me lick the bowl, mixers, and spoon. At ten, I knew how to clean greens, snap peas, and just plain damn cook. Not just that, she taught me how to cook, clean, iron, wash and you name it. I was back at my home church New Mt. Moriah Missionary Baptist Church that I thought I missed until I was a permanent fixture at my Grandmothers house. I went to church on Sunday morning and evening service, Tuesday prayer, Wednesday Bible study and in the summer vacation Bible school. I swore once I got grown I was not stepping foot in another church. Yet, I know she was giving my life structure, she was shaping me up to be a woman and most importantly she did it because she loved me.

My grandmothers house had a long sidewalk from the driveway that sat right across the train tracks. One day I saw a beautiful shapely woman with big hips and a smile to die for. She had this little red head brown skinned *"bad ass"* little boy that I later found out was my nephew. We were 18 months apart. Apparently when my brother left for the Coast Guard he had left a package with him. She dropped him off with all his clothes. I am trying at ten years old to figure out where the hell he came from. My grandmother welcomed him in with loving arms and another chore for me. I had to watch his bad ass. We are close like brothers and sisters now, but I use to hate to see him coming. I caught my ass whippings and his because I did not stop him from getting in trouble.

Well, summer was over. It was time to go back home to my mom and my sister. I really missed them. Then I will never forget that tearful phone call. I thought I was going with Mama and all I can remember her telling me was that, *"She was not established enough at the time to let me come home and I had to go to school in Gary."* *"Why did my mother not want me then?"* That was all I could ask myself. What was more important than getting your baby girl home? After I hung up crying I remember my grandmother holding me. She did everything in her power to stop me from crying. I remember climbing in that high bed with my grandmother crying until I went to sleep.

After I had accepted that I was not going to see my mom for a year I just shut down and grasped the concept that it was going to be just her and me. My *"grandfather/ uncle"* had already passed and I think she needed the company. My Baby brother she raised had left for the Air force so my grandmother really loved the fact I was staying. I was her big girl. *"Wayyyyment! Pump the brakes!"* My nephew..., you remember, the red head son my brother had left when he went to the Coast Guard? Well, he had been picked up in the summer for a few weeks after he had come a month ago, but for some odd reason was now back at my grandmother's house. He was a pain in my ass. Well, guess what he was going to school with me. Talking about bad luck. That shit was so *"NOT BEAUTIFUL."* That boy was the *"Seed of Chuckie"* and I was responsible for his ass. *"Ugh!"* Well, sometimes we got along. *"NOT!"*

September was approaching and my grandmother was not a last minute woman. In Gary, the main shopping strip was on Broadway...*YEAHH!* Like *"George Benson"* would sing *"On Broadway."* My grandmother couldn't drive so we caught the bus. It picked us up right in front of her house. My nephew and I loved Broadway in Gary, it was the most exciting thing in town and then after that we would go and see my favorite aunt on Connecticut Street. See getting lost in Gary was not easy to do. On one side of Broadway, the streets were named after the Presidents. On the other side where the famous *"Jackson family"* use to reside on Jackson Street that side of Broadway, the streets were named after the states in the New Colony and Connecticut was where my Aunt Rosie stayed. The realest old lady to kick it with, but my grandmother rarely let me spend the night there because Aunt Rosie spoiled the kids with a lot of fun and the corner store was our hang out and my grandmother did not like us far from her at all.

I remember at ten the corner storeowner had a basement and he threw the kids a basement blue light party before school. I had so much fun I could not sleep that night, but my grandmother never found out, *"LOL."* Aunt Rosie was cool! That whole summer we shopped on Broadway. My grandmother knew a man at a store and he was the owner. He was a nice white man named Mr. Miller. Back then we would shop like maniacs. I got whatever I wanted and my grandmother was so big in Gary that she never had to pay with cash. He would write it down on paper with a pencil. It was that way at all stores for my grandmother.

Later on, I found out, *"them clothes were not free."* Back then it was what they called credit. I wish it were that easy in this century. Credit was built on trust now you can't trust *"no damn body."* School shopping there was not like in Houston. We had to get extras, coats, boots, long johns, ski mask, and wool socks because a blizzard was guaranteed every winter.

Well, it was time for school. Welcome to Mary McLeod Bethune a school we walked to almost a half a mile from my grandmother's house. We were tired walking to school and tired coming back, but it made us tough and taught us independence at an early age.

CHAPTER 5
The Truth About Black History And My Life History

Growing up, I questioned a lot but was only comfortable and brave enough to ask my grandmother, because she just spit out the truth, no stuttering, no nothing. I had in early September, started attending elementary school and I had to watch my busy nephew. Even though he was busy I was very protective. My first day of school was not colorful it was just colored. There was not any other race in that school, but Black! Which was a great thing because I was young but yet interested in my race that was portrayed as *"NOT BEAUTIFUL,"* but was absolutely a rainbow of beauty. There were different shades of Black children, different hair textures and kids with boldness and full of life. Not only were they Black, they were proud of it. Me being a very light skinned, light eyed, red head little girl and my parents were both brown skinned. I often questioned my race, but I looked just like my grandmother and she stressed my ethnicity and her growing up in Mississippi. Her mom was light skinned, but her dad was a handsome dark skinned man. All of my grandmothers siblings were light skinned, hazel eyed, freckled faced and some handsome men and gorgeous women. That was my mom's family. I, later on, learned about my dad's family.

Mary McLeod Bethune Elementary, who was Mary McLeod Bethune? Well in the all-Black elementary school I was taught she was a strong Black woman that was an educator and civil rights activist that was known for starting private schools for African Americans. I learned I was at that time a part of greatness. She was a part of who I was. I also learned the national Black Anthem that was far better and more personal to me, who I was and why civil rights mattered. The song was called *"Lift Every Voice and Sing!"* Boy did we sing it.

Young gifted and black I was becoming and understanding why my family were such fighters. I believe my family should have been the poster board for Emiliano Zapata's quote, *"I'd rather die on my feet then to live on my knees"* because my family daily put up a fight for their Black community. You were not coming in Gary, Indiana to the suburban area of Marshalltown where my grandmother lived and run nothing. *"I WAS A PROUD BLACK SISTER!"* I learned a lot with my grandmother and at Mary McLeod Bethune. I had to be tough and speak my mind. I use to stare at the picture on my grandmothers wall of *"JFK," "MLK," and "RFK,"* and I would question my grandmother. She told me the stories of all three men assassinations and how they tried to give Black people a better life.

I then questioned my family history. The Tillman lineage and how I was a Stewart. Why did my daddy call my grandfather Uncle Bruce? Why did my mom call my dad's *"uncle"*, *"Daddy?"* Why did my brothers raised by my grandmother call her mama and called my mom by her first name? How was the man across the alley my uncle, which was my dad's brother? Even though things started out beautiful when I lived with my grandmother. The truth was coming out dammit, but not all the way. I also wanted to know how it was five siblings with one mother and five different last names, but only had three baby daddies. Man it was a cluster-fuck. Even my outspoken grandmother would change the subject to keep me from being young and lost. It still did not stop me from being lost, double kin and a child who was always told she was beautiful, but because of not knowing me for me I felt not so *"NOT BEAUTIFUL."*

My grandmother one day gave me some revelation on who I was, but I still was perplexed. She told me the man that I knew as my grandfather was her husband for over 30+ years and raised my mother, but he was her stepdad. My known grandfather who I knew and loved was my grandmother's second husband. Okay, are you sitting down? My mom's birth father was Eddie Wilson and he died from cancer and that is why my mom's maiden name is Wilson. So my now step-grandfather who raised my two brothers in my grandmothers and my step-grandfather's home which was my grandmother's husband of 30+ years home so he was the only daddy they knew so they called him Daddy.

Now the man across the alley was my uncle, he and my dad were brothers they called my mom's step-grandfather my step-granddad and my dad's biological uncle because that is what he was their uncle. Which made my grandmothers husband my biological uncle, Damn! Now this is how my mom and dad begat me. My grandfather uncle which was my paternal grandmother's brother had two nephews running from slavery in Mississippi to an uncle they had who took them in and he helped in finishing their upbringing. So my step-grandfather/uncle who raised my mom who was my dad's uncle came into play. My step-grandfathers, step-daughter had relations with his biological nephew and *"BAM! Here I am!"* *"A product of sheer bullshit."* If I was my parent's I would have hidden that shit from my child too. You will get it later. That explanation alone got me tired than a motherfucker.

Now I know why I could not go across the alley to my uncle's house and play with my cousins because my uncle was a fool. He would have told me a long time ago.

He said what it was, how it was and if you did not like it he would shoot you for not agreeing and questioning what the hell he was saying. I loved that man. My grandmother also had a son named Frank Brown, the coldest, coolest pastor that could preach and sing his tail off and after he preached he had his whiskey bottles in the back because he needed a drink. *"Don't judge my damn Uncle now!"* Noah was a drunk and they said God used him. So drop your *"over holiness."*

My Uncle kept it so real. We would ride in the car with him and when he hit the brakes you would hear all the rattling from the alcohol bottles clink clinking as he hit a stop sign, *"LOL."* Uncle was also a butcher/chef. He would smother the best roast and put carrots and potatoes around them and then tell you *"You Ain't Never Gone Eat A Possum That Damn Good!"* *"Barf!"* He was the chef at all family reunions so you would get full, but of what I do not know. I remember, as a child across from my grandmother's house was a train track and a field. My uncle kept a pistol and I heard shooting then here he come. This man had a dead rabbit, a pistol, and newspaper in hand. He skinned that rabbit, cleaned that rabbit, boiled and seasoned that rabbit and his country ass ate that rabbit. He was a character, but that is my history, my being and part of who I was.

I believe my mom had her own craziness that she was dealing with back in Houston. I know she loved me. She just was not ready for me. All her kids were adults except me and I was the baby, only ten years old. I am thinking she was taking a break from life. After all, I questioned her history with the men in her life and her five kids with different last names. I asked my grandmother one day. Why do we all have different last names? She began, *"Your two oldest brothers shared the same dad, but the oldest had your moms maiden name and the second brother got his fathers last name whom your mom was married too and he was a bigamist."* My Grandmother said, *"He was married to a woman in Vietnam."* She said, *"Even though your mom had a marriage license, it was no good."*

My next two siblings had the same Father. My third brother has the last name of another man my mom was fooling with because my brother and sisters dad was not acting right so she named him out of spite after the boyfriend, which later caused my brother a lot of hell. When my sister came along my mom made up with their dad. My sister was not conceived in anger so she hit the lotto and got her fathers last name, but she ended up hating her dad and loving mine because my dad was in her life more than her father. Now, I am not sure if it was voluntary or involuntary, but because of my poor mom getting her heart broke so much she probably kept my sister from her dad like she tried to with me, but it was not possible due to me being all up in the family. This mess was just what I said. A mess that was oh so *"NOT BEAUTIFUL."*

CHAPTER 6
Preparation Of A Young Adolescent

Well school was out. I was 11 years old then and my brother that was in the Air Force was sent from Germany back to the States and he had some time in between being transferred to Rapid City, South Dakota. He came to see the lady that he called mama. My grandmother. She could not have been happier to see the young boy she sent off from high school to the Air Force come back as a man. This time, he did not come back alone. He had a wife and two of the cutest little mini genius boys that would melt your heart away. Yeah! That's right I then had three nephews and one niece. My niece was from my second brother, but she rarely visited. I was a proud aunt. I had kids to boss around. That summer I thought I was going to Houston to be with my mom, but boy was I wrong. My brother and his wife did not know anyone in South Dakota and my nephews were like two and four. Guess who was in the car heading to South Dakota to babysit. You guessed it. ME! I started to feel passed around like a *"$2 whore"* by this family and the woman that could stop it had not seen her child going on a year and a half. *"This is bullshit!"*

I love my chubby chocolate brother. I remember him playing with me a lot as a little girl. I used to ride his back and would cry when he left to go anywhere. I will never forget. I was about four years old and my grandmother was in her favorite position at the front door in her chair sleep. My brother was in his room down the hallway just before you get to the kitchen, attempting to play the guitar. I snuck past both of them. At four I was slick. I went into the kitchen and climbed on the table, grabbed what I thought was sugar and it was a box of Morton's Salt. I grabbed it like a Colt 45 and chugged it down my throat. It cut off my damn breath. My brother ran from the back, stuck his finger down my throat, got as much salt out my throat as he could and held me like I was his own child. My grandmother wanted to beat me, but I damn near killed myself. All she could do was hold me crying and as usual, grandmother soothed my little behind and rocked me to sleep. I don't think I ever told him, *"Thank You."*

Well, we are in dry ass South Dakota. Land of *"Mt. Rushmore,"* and the "Honkies." The only blacks you seen in South Dakota was the blacks on the Air Force Base. I just left *"Chocolate Town"* and ended up in *"Whiter than White"* cricket infested South Dakota. No Bullshit! It was more crickets than people. I was ready to just settle in. It was damn near a two day drive from Gary, Indiana, because every time my nephews seen a damn McDonald's sign we stopped. Jesus Christ! As of this day, I cannot tell you the last time I ate a hamburger from McDonald's *"YUCK!"* All the houses looked the same where my brother stayed on this large Military base. It had a pond stocked with trout and was very clean, but it was very White. I went from, *"Lift Every Voice and Sing,"* to *"The Home of the Free and the land of the Brave,"* two very different national anthems. I am glad that my grandmother taught me, *"The Lord's Prayer"* and the *"23rd Psalms"* before I left because, *"dammit I needed it!!!!"*

My brother was so happy he loved his new wife. Then was my first time meeting her. I had heard about her from my mom because when they had their first born the day before my birthday my mom was there, but she left too soon. My sister-in-law had went into labor while my mom was flying back to Houston from what I heard, talking about twisted. Anyway, I had also heard and seen pictures of the pretty curly head chocolate baby that was identical to my brother. I loved my nephew. He was cute and not just that, he was born a day before my birthday. At the time I was not too sure of this wife. *"Where he meet her at?"* Who was this woman my brother was giving all his love and attention too? *"Hellooooo! Over here!"* I was already fighting for my mom's attention and I had just left the only woman at the time I was positive loved me without a limit. I was an 11-year old girl that felt empty, alone, and so *"NOT BEAUTIFUL."* My brother had changed in my mind. She stole all his love from me and I had to get it back. He was my brother before he was her husband and baby daddy. She was nice to me, but I did not care. I did not know her. I knew my brother. I missed him for four years and I wanted to be with him and not with her.

My brothers played a father role in my life and she was taking that from me. I had been through so much in my childhood with all the molestations and feeling unloved because the person I wanted to be with was too busy for me. I had no trust for no man and my brothers were my world. *"I WAS BABYGIRL!"* Even in the midst of my brother having a family that was new to me. I can say he spread his love and he still told me he loved me, he squeezed my nose and he still kissed his baby sister like I was still his baby, but too many people were there. Was my insecurities stemming from not being protected as a child? It was deep. I just wanted to be loved period. I really believe that as of today up until last year, I would fight to be approved, validated and loved by people because of the tragedies in my life. Now I am cold-hearted and mean. *"I DON'T GIVE A FUCK ABOUT WHAT PEOPLE THINK NOR SAY AND WILL GET AGGRESSIVE!"* I pray that God changes me and through this book as I write I slowly feel a change, but don't test me.

My brother had me spoiled rotten. I could walk the military base and I met a lot of military brats on the base, but they were the worst kids in the world. They smoked, drank, had sex, fought over boys and they were my damn age. *"Noooo,"* I wasn't ready. Right next-door were some kids that cursed and fought their mom and did not respect no one, but their dad. Both parents worked though and these girls were hot up the ass. Their dad had a camper under his part of the shed of the four home unit and when their parents left there was some teenage boys that would come over and they would be doing Lord knows what in that trailer. I did not want to know. I just knew it was loud. One day one of those young military brat boys came over to try and talk to me, and my Brother ran his ass smooth off. He was very protective of his baby sister and was not having it. Now there was one girl my age on the base that was pretty cool. Her family was well structured. Her mom taught me how to fish on the military base and I got pretty good. I would rake in some trout. My friends mom also taught me how to clean the fish and cook them.

To win my brothers love, I would try to catch a lot of fish and I would come home and cook the fish along with the sides. My grandmother had already instilled cooking in my soul. So I was already a *"mini chef."* His wife was proud of me and complimented me a lot on the things I was good at, but I was not trying to feel her at that time. Sometimes I loved her when my brother would make me mad and sometimes I didn't and that is when she and my brother was all *"lovey dovey."* I was a typical spoiled 11-year old, *"My way or no way."* I will never forget all the boring days I had in South Dakota when my brother and wife would go off to work. I had to keep my spoiled nephew. One was mean as hell and the other was a crybaby.

I swore I would never have kids. This was too much. I was feeding and rocking babies to sleep at 11-years old. I could never seem to have a normal fun summer.

My brother and wife were very much into education and while I was there I was going to learn. South Dakota is a very interesting place, especially Rapid City. There is actually *"fools gold"* in the street and you can see it as you walk down the street. It was a beautiful place, more of a tourist city due to Mt. Rushmore, it was just cricket infested. I can honestly say by 11-years of age I had already been in at least 25 states in the US if not more. My siblings were going to make sure I was the smartest kid on the block. US history was something I aced in school. I knew the states, the capitols of every state, what states started with what alphabets from the east coast to the west coast and even in Canada. I was sharp. I had no choice, but to know my brothers did not play. I even knew all the presidents. I remember when my brother and wife got a free weekend they took me to Mt. Rushmore and I knew, and I mean I had better knew every president on that monument. The pressure of education was put on me. Probably why I hate school now. Don't judge me. It was going on two months on that damn military base and I started to get bored and busy.

My brother had eventually put my nephews in daycare and I was wide open to fuck up. I start being cool with those nasty girls next door. I first picked up a bad cigarette habit, then I start talking to boys. I wasn't sexually active, but I seen a lot of sex next door. I was not doing that. I was a *"tomboy"* and I would have knocked the shit out of a boy, but I did put on makeup until my brother got home and talk to a boy, but he better had not touched me. I was only seeking at that time the love from my brother. He helped take care of me at my grandmother's house. I knew him and he protected me. I still wasn't feeling this wife thing though and then one day he set me straight! I tried to play my brother against his wife. I had made up lies about things she did that was not true and I was snappy with her. Who the hell did she think she was? I was going to break this marriage up at any means necessary. I was a mean 11-year-old kid. I knew how to conjure up some shit just to get attention and have my way.

Anyway, when my brother caught me rolling my eyes at my sister-in-law he spanked me. It hurt my soul. Why did he love her more than me? I hated her then. I was ready to leave that place. My brother then told me he loved me, but this was his wife and mother of his kids and if I tried to stir up anymore shit, he was going to spank me again. I knew then he spanked me out of love and I shaped up quick. I learned to love my new sister-in-law and accept that she loved me because she loved my brother. I never forget she got a job at a local mall in Rapid City and she took me shopping. We were best of friends. Now I think about it, why was I tripping? I was the only little girl in the house. All along I made my own life hard, but after not feeling loved by my parents at that time and watching my brother pour all his love into this new woman. I felt ugly, I felt empty. For some reason, I felt so *"NOT BEAUTIFUL!"* I just took what I could get out of love not really sure at that point what love was. I was so confused yet I made amends with my sister-in-law. They are still married as of right now and I love her too pieces. That summer I cried when I left and had to get on an airplane and head back to Houston. Finally....It was time for my mom to spend time with her own child.

CHAPTER 7
Return To Sender

Finally, I am back with my mom. Wow, she must have needed time to really get her life on track. She looked amazing. I landed in Houston from a long year being away from my Mom. She was doing really well. She had a house, a great paying job as a supervisor at the largest airport in Houston and she had a new found spirituality with God. She found her a church home in our new neighborhood. The name of the neighborhood Lakewood, Texas was mixed with blacks and whites that all worked at pretty good jobs and were raising great kids, to later on become something in life. Well before it was Lakewood it was Clairmont Place but now called Lakewood. I believe they changed it to the name of the church in the neighborhood that my mom happily attended. The Pastor of Lakewood Church was a great man and did a lot for the community and the kids in the community. We would walk to the nice yellow building on East Houston Rd. Actually, a lot of people walked in the neighborhood to this church. It was rare to find a white man that preached better than the pastor at my home church in Gary, Indiana.

I loved my mom's new life and her change for greatness. Yet in her eyes what she did to cover up her past did not work for me. My mom's eyes were literally the windows to her soul. I admired my mom. Her flesh had been crushed and some of her soul, but she remained focused and was determined to build a home in Houston for her family. At my new home was Mom, my sister, my two older brothers and I. If you remember, when we first moved to Houston on the Southside that Hill man that was 10 years older than my sister was still lurking around. He was pretending to be there for my older brothers, but I seen clean through him. He was after my then 16-year old sister. Had we had enough from older men lurking after my sister and me? The strange thing about this man though was he was accepted by my family, but he had a motive. He was hunting at 26, my sister who was just 16 and he would not stop until he got her. This was a sick, yet determined individual. There were women his age that was after him, but he was determined to be my sisters first everything.

He took her to school, he gave her money, and too much damn attention if you ask me. *"Was I the only one seeing this shit?"* Anyway, he got so into my sister's head that it had gotten out of control. My mom did intervene and she at this point did everything in her power to keep her from this man. My mom began to hate this man. She used to try to talk to my sister, but at 16, it is hard to start trying to teach a girl that age anything. Her ears then were closed and he had her head open. My sister would sneak off with this man when my mom was working. She was even skipping school then and spending time with him. My mom was fed up. She called my grandmother in Indiana and told her all the stuff that was going on. It had to be going on for quite a while. My sister had been hurt so much by men and she sought love so desperately as I did she let this old man give her this false sense of love. I also believe that because of him being so much older and her not having a father in her life at all. She felt a paternal bond as well as a passionate love for this Cat.

Well since my mom could not stop it. She and my grandmother decided to put her on an airplane and send her thousands of miles away from this older man to Gary, Indiana, but it was too late. A few weeks after being in

34

Indiana with my grandmother my mom got a call. My sister was...yes, you guessed it...pregnant for this older man that she sought love and attention from and hated my mom from separating them. The damage was done. My sister at 16 was a dropout, rebellious as hell and pregnant. My mom, I guess felt a little guilty about what happened and she did not want anymore anger from her two daughters to bring her more guilt so she made a decision. It may have been a wrong decision, but my mom was in the bonding stage with her two girls and she had begun spoiling us a lot.

My mom did not want my sister to hate her. After all, look at what she had been through. So my sister was pregnant, back on a plane to Houston and with welcoming arms from my mom. My mom did what she thought was best and she wanted my sister happy, so she signed the paperwork and finally that old bastard got what he wanted. My sister was a 16-year-old pregnant bride that had dropped out of school. Talk about some fucked up decisions being made. Yeah, it was some bullshit and my Sister had not even lived the life of a normal teenage girl. That Hill Dude had won and talking about a so *"NOT BEAUTIFUL SITUATION!!!"* I know my poor mom was crushed, but her hands were tied. All she could do was cry and pray for her oldest naive daughter seeking love from a man and not a forced sexual abuse, but definitely a mental manipulation by an older man that played my *"Whole Got Damn Family."*

CHAPTER 8
Grade School

East Houston Elementary was the name of the closest elementary school in Lakewood. I entered in the 4th grade. I never remember walking through the doors with my mom scared as hell. Even though we lived in a then nice neighborhood, Lakewood, not all the kids were so fortunate. I was blessed to have all new everything and a mom who believed that we were not leaving out her house looking any kind of way because it was a reflection of her. Some of those poor kids raised themselves. This was a lot different from the other elementary schools I had attended. When I first got to the school, I heard the year before this little boy and his brother were playing in the curve that was on the road before the school. Well, one of the brothers was playing in the rain with a trash bag on his head running in and out of traffic and all of a sudden he was hit and tragically killed.

So that particular school year kids had already been struck with a tragedy, grief and some with poverty. I felt so bad for those kids. I use to take things from home and give them away just to help the kids have nice things like myself. If my mom would have known, then she would have killed me. She worked hard, but I didn't at the time know the value of money because I was so spoiled. I had my mom, grandmother, three older brothers with a job and a sister with a husband who had a good job. I wanted for nothing I was blessed. Yet some of the kids at school when you looked at how they came to school you could tell that their lives were not as great as mine.

NOT BEAUTIFUL

First week of school, my mom had to work and I had to get to school so she put me on a private bus. Most of the kids whose parents worked and came from my side of Lakewood could afford to ride private buses. The school at the time did not have a public bus to bring the not so fortunate kids to school, they had to walk. I hated to see those poor kids walking in all climates of weather, but for some strange reason, I wanted to walk too. I hated that *"Big Fat Ass"* mean bus driver. Then she was so money hungry, kids would have to sit on the floor to all fit in that damn hot box van she called a bus. I hated to hear her coming in the morning to my house yelling and shit. She was so fat the front end of the bus scrubbed the street. She had to pile most the kids in the back of that bus/van to even it out for a safe ride to school.

I met my fourth-grade teacher and she was a mean heifer too. This was not at all like the close-knit neighborhood I went to school at in Gary. Plus education wise I was ahead of all the kids in my class. Kids were all over the place. They were bad as hell. I guess if the teacher wasn't mean we would have ran her over, because every time that lady left the room, class turned into a zoo!! I had never seen so many mannish little boys in my life and the little girls, *"wer fass as hell!"* I was not use to this shit. When I got to that school I got my boxing game up so hard that *"Mayweather"* didn't have shit on me. When the teachers would turn their heads boys were grabbing girl's booty. I will never forget this little badass nappy head boy grabbed my behind and I beat him good. He must have loved the way I'd beat him because he did not stop grabbing me and I did not stop beating him. I was real quiet in school. I really had no friends.

Then one day I ran into this pretty little girl in school nicknamed Rabbit. She lived directly behind the school in a great big house. It had to have at least five rooms and three bathrooms. It was her grandparent's house, but her entire family lived there. We became best friends. Even though she lived right behind the school her paw-paw would bring her to school in his fine automobile. One day I was waiting for the fat nasty mean bus driver when Paw-Paw seen I was Rabbit's best friend so he took me home that day. I loved being at Rabbit's house. She had all the latest toys, clothes, and they had *"CABLE!!"* We didn't have cable at my house. It wasn't like we couldn't afford it. My mom would spend money on me, but cable, *"was the devil."* Paw-Paw had me and Rabbit so spoiled we would just go to the back of the school and cut across those woods to Rabbit's house. Paw-Paw knew our favorite movie too. *"The Incredible Shrinking Woman!"* We watched it over and over again.

My mom finally met Paw-Paw and her and Rabbit's mama became the best of friends. For the first time in my life, I could spend the night away from home. I no longer rode that fat mean ladies bus. Paw-Paw told my mama he would pick me up and take me to school every day. That was exactly what he did. Me and Rabbit rode to school together all the way up to high school. We were what they call now ride or die!

CHAPTER 9
Becoming Of A Young Woman

Later on after we finished the fifth grade at East Houston Elementary. Of course I finished with A/B Honor roll because I was so much more advanced when I moved back to Houston. All the kids that I went to school with were all transferred to the same middle school R.E Kirby Middle School. It was an experience. We were 6th graders and when I got there a lot of the girls were so much more experienced and their bodies were developed like grown women. I was a beautiful, yet shy adolescent and at that time in my home, I was already told no boys and no makeup until I was 15. My mom was determined not to make the same mistake in my life that was made with my sister. I was going to do something with my life.

My 6th-grade year was trying. I never tried to blend in I was not a group type individual, but I was pulled in by the young light skin girls at the school. See the way it was in the south at that time, the light skin black girls hung with the lights and the dark skin girls hung with the dark and it was conflict between the two. *"It was crazy!"* Kinda like in the slavery days where the light skinned women worked in the house and the dark skinned girls picked cotton. Enslaved and very shallow, there was a prejudice in my own race. Had they not heard that the south was free on June 19th and that we were not segregated, not unlike up North I had never seen such behavior.

Even with the teachers, the lighter children were treated better than the dark skin children. A prejudice taught

41

at a young age and a bunch of sheer ignorant individuals. It was a lot of lighter kids too because a lot of them had family that came from Louisiana which according to history was conquered by the French and was stolen by America and slaves had been brought in by the white man and the children came from French descent. A lot of beautiful people, but no different than my family we were descendants of the French, and Indians and they migrated to the South to Mississippi and worked as slaves. Raped by the white man, my descendent were light skin, freckled face, green-eyed individuals. My family of course left the South in the 1900's to give us a better life up in Gary, Indiana/Steel town is what they called it and we owned everything we worked for. As in the late 1900's in the South the slaves were not aware they were free until Juneteenth, yet forced to celebrate July 4th, Independence Day which is not independence day for the South. Yet America lied then and it is 2015 today and the lies are even thicker. *"SMH!"*

Sixth grade was actually fun, I was in the band and a cheerleader. Yet very quiet a lot of the kids knew me, because of my upscale upbringing and mannerism. Rabbit and I were still the best of friends and later on I befriended two other ladies who were as goofy and shallow about being young adolescent girls as Rabbit and me. It was rough being a 6th grader in school. We had to deal with mannish 8th-grade boys. Yes, they preyed on us like wolves on a bear and we had to fight. Back then me and my new friends were determined to maintain our virginity, but some other, *"fass little girls, were giving it up like stuffing on Thanksgiving."* I knew little about sexual experiences in the sixth grade. I was sheltered. I remember as a child in my 8th-grade year I was climbing a tree as most tomboys did and I was so rough my mom kept Band-Aids.

On that day playing with my friends that lived

across the street from me, I went to use the restroom and I had blood in my panties. I was terrified. I ran home and told my mom I was climbing a tree and I cut my cootie. I never forget the *"OH SHIT"* look on her face, time for *"the talk."* It was a thing she said was a period and she was not talking about, *"English."* I was so damn afraid and the Band-Aid she gave me for that cut was 40 times larger than the Band-Aids she had when I would fall down. Talking about confused. Mama told me bits and pieces about it and said when you are on your period I could not even take a bath I was like, *"WTF?" "Why Mama,"* I asked? She replied, *"Because your not supposed too."*

I was devastated and they did not have sexual education in school in the 80's. I did what I knew best I called 219-885-8039. You damn right I called my *"Gangsta Grandma"* and she told me some stuff about being a woman that I was not trying to hear. When she said this shit was coming every month and do not let no one touch me on it, because it was contagious, so she told me *"LOL!"* She had to fabricate some. The pregnant part about if you did not have one came up about 4 years later. I at that point in my life guarded my cootie like I was in the penitentiary and had dropped the damn soap. Yet there were some girls who would talk about sex and their periods as if it made them popular, but it made them sound like *"$2 hookers."*

Back at Kirby Middle School, it was surrounded by apartments and a neighborhood called the *"HOLE,"* boy was it rough. Well that was where the sexual festivities took place for the mannish boys and hot girls. Wow! I was afraid to let some one touch my cootie especially with what had happened in my childhood experiences that still haunted me, yet alone let a mannish little boy put his stuffing in me. It was creepy. I remember the 8th-grade girls wore makeup, had boyfriends, kissed boys in the hallways, held hands

43

walking each other to class, passion marks, and where in the hell did the passion come from at that age. All of the girls were not like that. We did not go near those apartments with those nasty boys. *"YUCK!"*

Growing up in middle school though was not half bad, especially on the weekend. We had an amusement park called Astroworld and it was the shit. I was 14, so during my 8th-grade summer getting ready for my 9th-grade year Mom gave me some rope. Astroworld held concerts for the hottest groups back then, but I was a die hard NEW EDITION FAN. All of the concerts were held on the hill. It used to be Whodini, The Fat Boys, Lisa Lisa and the Cult Jam, LL Cool J, and too many other groups to name. I mean if your Mama bought you a season pass you were a Baller. Every Saturday me and my friends rode the bus to Astroworld. It was the 77 Liberty to the 9 Hirsch and that made us independent. We were live then with our jams and tank tops. You couldn't tell us we were not the shit. Back then the jheri curl was out.

Everyone had one, but not me. My mama was not processing my hair. I so envied the other kids that had one, because "Michael Jackson" had one and he was the man then too, but you did not have to worry about him coming to Astroworld. Back then I was a "Prince" fan more so. I had more Prince paraphernalia then MJ. I got into a fight in middle school about Prince. Prince made a movie called *"Purple Rain"* with "Appolonia," and "Morris Day and the Time", but I was Appolonia. Yes I was a *"Sex Shooter"* and did not know what the hell that song meant nor *"Darling Nikki"* either but I was Appolonia. Yet he was not coming into Astroworld, so I stuck with my New Edition, oh yeah and "Jazzy Jeff and The Fresh Prince." If I knew then what I knew now Jada would have been in trouble. *"Lol!"*

Chapter 9

Some weekends Astroworld did not have a concert, so we would go to one of the largest skating rinks on the Northside called Super Skate. Now being that my other Grandmother lived in a home in the neighborhood called *"the Hole,"* we could just cut across the trail. There was also a movie theatre right next door to the skating rink, but we rarely went there, only in the summertime during the week when the skating rink was closed. If I tell you on Saturdays we skated from noon until midnight. That was the spot. We would also have skating groups and on dance night, we had dance groups. This was during the Crush Groove break dancing era so everyone knew how to pop lock. I knew boys that walked around with cardboard boxes just so they could show off their break dancing skills. Now do not get it twisted. I was in a girl group that danced and I could out pop lock some of the fellas, sometimes I did talent shows with the fellas. Yes, dancing was something I loved to do. Life was fun and innocent.

Now back to the skating rink. We would have dance contest and dance night, but not too much dancing was going on when the lights went out and the disco lights came on. I believe that was at that time I discovered my hormones. I use to watch girls and boys do what we called back then *"screwing."* I was afraid to do it because Mama said screwing would get me pregnant, but I had a crush on a popular boy that was a little older and fine. He constantly played with me, but I had no experience in nothing. I did not even know how to kiss. I dreamed about it, but I dare not do it, *"I ain't want no baby."* Especially after in the eight grade one of the girls got pregnant. The most we did was conversate and hold hands. He was advanced and I know he wanted to do the screw. Of course, at the skating rink, it was with all our clothes on. *"He He!"* Now I know as an adult the kids were not doing nothing, but if not for people being there we would have had more than one pregnant 8th grader.

I could not do it though. I was molested so much as a child sometimes if a boy touched me I would slap the shit out of him. I was very protective of my body. I was especially protective because I had start growing in areas that I did not see coming. I was the little girl in the 8th grade that had no problem having a little boys nose wide open because I was absolutely even more beautiful than that little girl that left Gary, Indiana, but for some reason because of all the sick perverted things that happened to me as a child I just felt oh so *"NOT BEAUTIFUL"* at all. Nope, I saw nothing good about my self!

CHAPTER 10
Teenage High

Welcome to high school. It was huge. Not like elementary or middle school. As we walked into the large campus we were immediately recognized as *"FRESHMEAT!"* Especially to the senior boys at my new high school. I had recognized some of the older kids that were much older than I at my new school. In that predominantly black school district, it was approximately four middle schools. I had been split up from my other friends from my middle school, therefore; I was this young, beautiful, long hair light skinned girl who had to walk those big halls by myself. I was not the only big thing walking. The football players, mostly senior boys, had a hallway, which they stood at and in between classes I dreaded walking down that hallway.

Those boys would grope and touch us and playfully pin us girls up against the wall, but after all, I had been through in my younger life it was not a game. I would be terrified. Well until I found a shortcut to miss that hallway or would run like hell through that one. I began to wonder, "Why were these boys so damn perverted?" Not all of them, though. My ninth grade year I attracted one of the finest senior gentlemen a young girl could meet. He was not like those other guys, he was my friend. He would carry my books to class even if he was late for his, he would walk me to my bus after school and then he got a car. Still yet a gentleman he would drop me off in Lakewood, but I would not let him drop me off at home. I was just 14 in the 9th grade. If my mom found out she would kill me.

I had missed my middle school friends especially Rabbit, Nona, and Ursala. They had split us up and we only got to see one another at lunch, after school, and on weekends. Yet we had a lot to talk about at our new high school. We were maturing quickly, but not as quick as *"those big booty, big breasted"* junior and senior girls they were built like *"Pam Grier"* well some of them anyway. Some were built like something I refuse to give a name. Let's just say it was an awful mess *"LOL."* We all had what we called crushes. You know the things that only best friends knew about, but the boys we were crushing had no clue. Yet I was still that *"Tomboy"* that picked up my boxing game from up north, yet I was becoming a teenager and a young lady, but God forbid if my mama was gone make me wear a dress.

I had enemies for no reason just because I was cute with a nice build. *"You know!"* Like I do now. Back then we called them bitches, now we have given them the crown word called *"HATERS"* and now I am grown I could give *"2 shits"* about them. Most of them bought this book just to be nosey and I'd like to take a minute to *"THANK ALL MY HATERS! KMSL."* Yes, I am a clown and at my new school that is when my popularity kicked in. I was a miniature *"Richard Pryor"* who was so silly that there was not a principal in that school back then that did not know me nor my rear end. In high school corporal punishment was real or, call *"Yo Mama."* I would let the Principle beat my ass for $500. Just do not call my Mama. Then that was two ass whippings in one day.

I had met some pretty tough friends in school added to my other friends that I had grown up with. They were *"Tomboys"* too and once they seen my boxing game on the campus we had turned into a mini-gang. I started to skip class, was at every lunch and would fight my ass off. I also picked up at age 14, a marijuana habit, a heavy marijuana habit. In spite of all I did though, I was an honor student. All *"A's"*, in grades and all *"U's"*, for unsatisfactory in conduct. I was good though I had also picked up a hell of a report card forgery habit. My Mama didn't even know. I had established a name and character for myself. Yes everybody loved me. That boyfriend I had as sweet as he was I left him alone, besides I really had male issues and during that time kissing and holding hands was not my flavor.

During lunch, we had our own table. The *"athletes"* had theirs, the *"bougy chics"* had theirs, and *"us,"* we had *"ours and yours,"* and if you had a problem, believe we stayed *"ready to solve them."* We would go behind the building where the bus picked us up and would blaze. I will never forget, we got caught by a principal, and man we were scared, but this *"Nicca"* hit the joint. Fucked us up. From that point on to stay out of trouble with him, he smoked with us. I guess with all them bad ass black kids *"he neeeded to be high Shiddd!"* After we would smoke, *"maannn...,"* we could eat up some shit at lunch. Lunch was an hour and back then rap was getting more and more popular. I always had a thing with words. I could freestyle my ass off. I was killing girls and dudes no pen, no paper but what they did not know in my alone time all I did was read.

Yes, I was not what I was at school. Let's just say besides my boxing skills, people did not know I was very conscious minded. I was the *"great pretender."* In the library, I had seen great books. I was very intrigued about black history, Martin Luther King, Rosa Parks and many more. Yet this one book caught my eyes and I could not put it down. The *"AUTOBIOGRAPHY OF MALCOLM X!"* Yes in my home where my TV stayed on *"PTL"* and *"Jimmy Swaggart"* I picked up a book as such. I was very impressionable at that age and Malcolm X had put me in a place, and a world in a space and time where white people had become the enemy and Jesus was a myth. I knew then I had to hide this book. My mama was not going to entertain the thoughts of me questioning Jesus, the resurrection nor the Holy Trinity. Things that made me question all of my beliefs.

One day I believe my mother found that book because it mysteriously disappeared from the hiding spot in my room and I never saw it again. Yet I questioned anything about religion. If Jesus was a savior, why didn't he save me from being raped, abused, molested and not one person had suffered from what the hell they did making me feel as if I was *"NOT BEAUTIFUL?"*

CHAPTER 11
Daddy Where You.... And My
Hormones Come From?

By my junior year, I had got my stuff together. My conduct grades had changed due to the end of my sophomore year and I could not forge my report card, "no more." Second semester my grades had dropped and Mama found out when she got a letter from the school saying my English teacher failed me for the semester and I had to go to summer school at my mom's expense. That was an expensive class along with an *"ass whippin."* That summer in summer school, there were two high schools in our district and we all had to go to one school to fix what we had all fucked up. I really had no interest in boys but this one boy, *"OH MY GOD! OSCAR! WHERE IN THE HELL DID HE COME FROM?"* He had to attend the other school because I had not been attracted to no one at my high school like I was too him and Got Dammit, he had mutual feelings. By then my mom allowed me to date. I do not think a day went by that we had not seen one another. *"I WAS IN YOUNG LOVE!"* The whole school knew to and we did not give a damn.

That was the best summer ever and I looked forward to summer school. This boy had a mean ass dress code. His swag was just so *"Uhhhhh!"* I believe this brown skinned, big eyed, long lashes and his lips. Oh my goodness were so suckable. He was my first. We really both did not know what the hell we were doing. Well, that is what he told me. I was clueless! Yet eventually, we figured all that out. My mom worked all day at the Airport, but his mom was a hairdresser that had a shop at her home, so no privacy there. Yet he had a really cool dad that knew we were head over hills for one another.

I had no idea what *"French kissing"* was, but when I placed my lips on his. I was speaking in *"French Dammit!" "Polly Vu Fran,"* whatever that woman said. That kiss made me see fireworks in 110-degree heat and made my body feel something that a young girl was not supposed to feel. Well being Mama was at work, we had the house all to ourselves. That kiss led to touching. I boldly went to touch him and he had a print in the jeans the size of an anaconda. I was thinking *"Oh Lord please help me,"* I was ready but I wasn't ready! That boy was either working with something, or I was just new to the different shapes, sizes and sculptures to the penis.

We kissed and we touched places on one another that I know for a fact on my body that had not been yet touched. Yet for him to be a young 16-year old boy he was taking it nice and slow. He slowly unbuttoned my shirt and undid my bra. I thought only babies sucked breast. I thank the Lord Mama lied to me about why I was on birth control pills and regulating my cycle because my body was doing shit that I did not even know worked on my young yet tender body. I was saying *"Hallelujah"* and it was nothing Holy about what was about to go down. He made me feel so good that all of the trauma in my life slowly faded away because I loved this boy and I knew that he loved me. He began to slowly lick my breast... *"Jesus what was that electricity that had just went through my body?"*

In my innocent mind, we did not pay the light bill because *"my lights was off"* and my body, *"was turned on!"* He slowly caressed both of my breasts slowly nibbling, kissing, sucking and caressing them in a way that as I type and reminisce I cannot explain. Then he began to lick below my breast. *"WTH?"* I knew about sex education, well what they taught at school and a little biology, but this was not in not one *"DAMN BOOK!"* He began to kiss my belly button and he slowly lifted up and off my skirt. He began to kiss my thighs and I shook like never before. If you would not have known any better I was having a damn seizure. Then all hell broke loose.

This boy placed his lips on my secret garden. I was oozing in ecstasy. His penis was rock hard, but he was not selfishly worrying about himself he was focused on pleasing me. He slowly licked my vagina. I moaned in soprano and I have always had a deep voice, but *"El Debarge"* was an amateur compared to how he sucked on my vagina or should I say *"my pussy."* I was so wet you would have sworn I was nine months pregnant and my water bag had just bust. By then I was ready for everything. He slowly and gently placed that anaconda inside my vagina. I had about *"20 orgasms"* so ready was an understatement.

He went in and it was painful yet I wanted him inside of me so like a gangsta I sucked up that pain. Once he broke me in and he began stroking in and out of me, kissing and looking me in my eyes. We both simultaneously said, *"I LOVE YOU!"* Most women say that their first time was horrible, but I cannot tell you that lie. As he went in and out of my pussy I began to love him more, and, more with each delicate stroke. Then I felt his penis tightening inside of me and he moaned in a way that I had never heard a man moan before and then he screamed! I felt an explosion inside of me that I had never experienced in my life. He kept screaming beautiful thing to me, and *"I LOVE YOU"* over and over again. It was the most beautiful feeling in the world. For once a man not taking my body, but I gave myself away *"I FELT BEAUTIFUL"* and I wanted everything he gave to me. He made me *"feel beautiful."*

We rolled over and it was natural as we held one another. I glanced over at the alarm clock on the side of my bed and I jumped up. *"OHHH SHIT!"* Mama get off at 2 pm and is home by 3 pm and it was 2:45. *"I LOVE YOU, but you got to get the HELL OUTTA HERE!"* He got dressed and there was a corner store by my house in Lakewood he called his dad and he picked him up there. Damn that was close. He called me later on and I couldn't stop laughing yet blushing because of the event that took place that day. *"I WAS A WOMAN"*…Well I had committed my first woman act at 16 years old. We would fall asleep on the phone with sweet *"I LOVE YOU's"* and we did that for almost a year and then as time progressed so did my experience in sex and in boys or should I say, men.

One day while sitting at home alone after school I get a knock at the door. Even though at 16 I was home in the afternoon by myself my mom was really strict about opening her door when she is not at home. I still always looked out the window and let in my friends and threw them out an hour before Mama would get home. On this day, I looked out the door and it was a well-dressed man with a dob on and he was very familiar looking. Despite of what Mama said I opened the door. I screamed, *"Daddy!"* Yes my daddy had found us again, but this time, it was no taking your child and running I was a teenage girl that was old enough to make my own damn decisions.

"Daddy, how did you find us?" He replied *"Your Grandmother Baby."* See my grandmother was never for my mom treating me the way she treated my dad and used me as a pawn. That is when I promised to myself that when I had children no matter how trifling their daddy was I was not taking that privilege from them. I was going to let them

make that decision on their own. Daddy was all smiles. He looked as though he was in tears, he finally got back his baby girl but I was not a baby though. I asked him, *"Daddy where have you been?"* He replied, *"Looking for you."* I was in awe. I had no clue that my father stayed away because he could not find me. I thought that it was because it was for selfish reasons and that made me feel so *"NOT BEAUTIFUL,"* but all of that about my dad was a lie. He was not a sorry man that did not care. He was a man who had lost his daughter because of all the bad things he did to my mother and I was her form of punishment.

"DAMN!" Well all that did not matter I had my daddy back. I remember my sister who lived directly across the street from my mother coming through the door. Boy was she happy to see Daddy. Well to this day, the only daddy she says she ever knew. Yeah she was on the run with Mama and I. My grandmother always kept it real. She was not a bitter woman. She believed in *"FAMILY"* and she knew I needed my daddy. See I had a taste of life. I was sexually active, smart and determined that I was not taking *"no more ass whippings"* from my mom who I held a strong bitterness towards. See to me, just because you removed us from the pedophiles and moved us to Houston. You were still in communication with that part of the family and for that, I had a hate deep in me that I could not let go.

I felt if she had stayed with Daddy none of this shit would have happened, because even though Daddy was who he was, he took care of me. Yeah he drank a lot, smoked a lot, gambled a lot and he was a garden tool. Back then my grandmother and her sister's husbands were too, but they did not divorce. I do not even remember my grandparents arguing. I was taught though by Grandma, *"You don't miss ass, you miss money, that is his ass let him do what he want with it, but that check was coming home."* When I say, *"until death due us apart,"* my family did not know what divorce papers were and still did what a wife was supposed to do and that was take care of home and her husband.

My mom could not stand my dad, but at 16 what was she going to do, but be just that *"MAD!"* She would try to keep me from Daddy, but not this time. If I had to run away and several times I did to be with my father I was calling my daddy. He loved me and kept it real with me. Yet he spoiled me in the wrong way. We smoked weed together, we drank together, we shot pool together and he had my pimping skills on *"FLEEK!"* Yes I was a player at 16. My mama was so sick of us she let him have my ass. Finally, a home without all them fucking rules, me and Daddy were inseparable, we were ride or die. He had got us an apartment off this street on Antoine and across the street was a Showbiz Pizza. Yes I got my first job with my Dad. I still had to go to school though. That was one thing my parents agreed on.

My mom still had a lot of say so in my life though and I was a Tomboy, plus Daddy would always remind me, *"That's yo Mama!"* *"Ugh!!!!!!"* One weekend I will never forget, my mom was determined to get that Tomboy out of me so she took me to this place called *"BARBIZON SCHOOL OF MODELING!"* *"Daddy, HELP!"* I could not win on that shit. I needed a *"joint,"* a *"Jack Daniels Down Home Punch,"* and some *"DICK!"* This was torture. I was at that school a whole year as a matter a fact, my whole damn junior year. Hell I was in the drill team at my high school and I shook my ass every Friday night, wasn't that enough? I was busy at 16, I was in high school drill team practice every day after school and modeling school all weekend and once a week, plus I had a damn job. Finally my junior year, I obtained a degree in modeling and my time was freed up a little. *"Thank You GOD!"*

It had been some months that Daddy had been in Houston, he was settled in working for the City of Houston where he later retired and was helping raise me. I was working with my dad and one day he went into father mode. He told me, *"You working now and getting older, time for responsibilities."* *"WTH?"* He had to be getting cool with Mama. I replied, *"Daddy Responsibilities?"* Yes, *"RESPONSIBILITIES!"* I will never forget the day Daddy handed me a light bill. I started to not like his ass then, who the hell did he think he was? *"Nigga you just showed up, now you wanna raise a motherfucker?"* *"Okay!"* I dropped out of drill team and found my own extra curriculum activities.

Back in High School we had only two schools in our district and we were rivals, but I was always attracted to older boys and boys from the rivalry team at Forest Brook. Well at one game I met a young very dark skinned dude who had graduated the year before. We started dating and it was getting intense. I would sometimes skip school just to be with him and had mastered writing a letter of absence, but he was a *"Man"* and made my ass go to school. He had a truck so all the bullshit was a rap. He had a job at the airport as a bartender and he would give me damn near his whole check so Showbiz Pizza was as good as quit! Huh! I had a *"Man"* with a car and a job. He was actually preparing for our future. My dad met him one night. I will never forget, I was getting dressed one night and I was in my room. I heard the knock on the door, but I also heard the door *SLAM!*

My daddy told him I wasn't there and slammed the door in his face. My beeper immediately went off! I knew *"Daddy Lil Mean Ass"* did something. This man was a mess. Eventually, we went on our date, but he was scared shitless of my gun packing crazy ass Daddy. He was the definition of *"GOT DAM FOOL."* Look in the dictionary you will find his picture. On weekends, I would go to my mothers and with me being away so much she missed me dearly. Daddy big mouth ass told her I had a boyfriend. My mom had a lot of questions and she had heard he was financially taking care of me. It was going smoothly until she met him.

My mama was on the phone when he pulled up and I said *"Bye Mama!"* She said, *"Oh hell nawl tell him nobody honks no horn for my daughter. Tell him, get his ass out that truck!"* *"Oh LAWD!"* So as she stayed on the phone gossiping he came in and spoke. That red woman got off the phone and was shocked as hell. *"YES!"* My mama was *"color struck"* and he was *"black as smut!"* I had went against the *"color code."* I am *"LMAO"* now! I always went against the grain. She had to stare at this *"dark, dark man,"* for five minutes. She questioned him on that night about her daughter. He was very charming and charismatic, plus he was buying shit for me that freed up her money.

We dated almost a year and he told me he had did something and wanted to talk to me. I was prepared, yet I had something to tell him. We had spent some *"Beautiful times"* together especially Valentine's Day and during that time was Mardi Gras and we had a room at this hotel off of Galveston Beach the month before and we had sex on a regular. So that night what he told me was he wanted me to be his wife and had the biggest ring a 16-year-old girl had ever had, but he had bad news at the same time. He told me he was joining the Army. I cried furiously, because what I had to tell him was bittersweet. I looked at him with tears in my eyes and I told him *"I AM PREGNANT!"* He immediately as a real man started making plans in his head. He was leaving for Oklahoma in two months and we were going to get married before he left and I was approaching my senior year in high school, not to mention my parents were going to kill me, but he was not for that abortion shit!

Two months had passed and all I can remember was the night before he was getting picked up to leave for the Army. Tears all night for he and I. All the fun we had all summer before he left, Deussen Park, high school football games and Love. The morning the Army came to pick up my man I cried a river. It was me, his parents, his siblings, cousin and his best friend. The saddest day of my life I had to go through a pregnancy all by myself *"DAMN!"* I missed him already. I had an *OH SO "NOT BEAUTIFUL,"*experience.

CHAPTER 12
Pregnant, Young And Afraid

Well he was gone and months were passing by. I was getting ready for my senior year in high school. I kept my pregnancy very private. I didn't start showing until my 7th month of pregnancy, *"SURPRISE!"* My baby's father and I talked every day and his mom and my mom made sure he played a part in my pregnancy as if he was here in Houston. Plus his dad and mine spoiled me to death. Man his father could cook. A man from DeQuincy, Louisiana and he had the accent to fit. He would fight for me with his wife about everything. I oh so miss him. Anyway because my boyfriend and his mother had something in common and that was the LOVE for her son. I guess God had a conversation with her because for some odd reason we start getting along. We were glued at the hip. She and my mom both took me to the doctor and over-fed me. I had a wonderful pregnancy.

Well three months was over and Army Boot Camp was over. I was preparing to see, *"My Heart, My Love, My Childs Father."* I was on my way to Oklahoma to watch him graduate. This was one of the happiest days in my life. My tummy had started to do this fluttering thing and my life was good to me. I will never forget the drive and the anticipation of seeing *"MY MAN."* Other than the frequent *"pee-pee,"* stops his mom had to keep pulling over to make, it was a great trip. Finally, we had arrived. You talking about a jumping pregnant woman and a kiss that in my mind no one seen but us and oops his mama seen us, *"Lol."* It was amazing but the sad thing is, it was a one-night stay. The most beautiful stay.

Then the next day after the graduation he had some news that was so *"NOT BEAUTIFUL!" "HE WAS GOING TO BE STATIONED IN GERMANY! ARE YOU FUCKING KIDDING ME!" "I will be 17 in a few months, and this baby is due in December so we have to get married when you come back and I had to have this baby without you!"* I stormed out that damn place! He followed quickly! *"What the hell was me and my baby supposed to do without YOU,"* I stated? He told me *"I will be in Houston for three weeks and we will figure this all out,"* but he promised me that *"FOREVER,"* was in our *"FUTURE!"*

For some reason, that was not good enough for me! So much ran through my mind! I just needed to be alone. *"THIS GOD I BELIEVED IN! Once again, God, you have failed me. Why do I pray? Why do I even give a fuck?"* Well, he was back in Houston for three weeks. It was like we had started to date all over again. He was strong, protective, but the best part was *"HE LOVED ME! I WAS CARRYING HIS CHILD. I LOVED THIS MAN WITH EVERYTHING IN ME!"* One weekend I will never forget he asked me to marry him before he left for Germany. I was 16, yet *"I SAID YES!"* We were very happy. We told my parents and family, yet when he told his parents his father was ecstatic, but that mama of his was not. I hated her and to this day. I hate her for interfering in something so beautiful that turned out to be oh so *"NOT BEAUTIFUL!"*

I remember these exact words from his mother's mouth, *"IF YOU MARRY HER YOU ARE DISOWNED FROM THIS FAMILY!" "WTH HAPPENED THIS WOMAN WAS JUST IN MY FACE AND NOW THIS."* I had never met a demon like her. It was a control thing with this woman over her sons. I believe that is why the oldest son moved to Atlanta. I could hear his dad tare into her ass! Then all of a sudden my child's father stormed out the door. I had never seen a man crying and as mad as he. In his heart and mind, *"HOW COULD SHE DO THIS TO ME?"* He only had three weeks in Houston before he moved out of the country for an entire year and a half. My Love for him could not and would not let his tears continue. I made him a promise. I told him when he got back, *"I would be here, the baby would be here, your SON WILL BE HERE!"* Yes we were having a *"BOY."* I seen a frown go upside down I made his night turn to day in a flash.

Well the three weeks had passed. Even though he was at odds and had a strong inside hatred for his mother we tolerated her. I was helping him pack and I went through his bags and what I found was *"UNBEARABLE!"* Seems like the, I am bored in Oklahoma shit was just that *"SHIT!"* I found pictures of him and other women partying as if he did not have a pregnant fiancé in Houston. Oh no Nigga, *"sitcho ass down!"* I got questions. *"The day before you leave the country this is the shit I see!"* *"DAMN!"* He sat there like *"MOST MEN"* looking stupid. His reply, *"Baby we celebrated after boot camp those are just women that they had on the base to party with."* I was so hurt, yet *"VENGEFUL!"* Fair exchange is not *"highway robbery."* *"KARMA IS A BITCH NIGGA!"*

Well my fiancé was on his way. Even though I forgave him! I could not forget. While I am over here crying and being faithful you were over there having a funky good time. I was hurt. Then after what his mother did, being my mother could be a *"SWEET DREAM OR A BEAUTIFUL NIGHTMARE, I STAYED THE HELL AWAY FROM THAT WOMAN."* Yet his dad never missed a day seeing me. I was carrying his grandson, but all he did was feed me. Eventually, I started to forgive his mom, *"OLD*

WITCH!" I had too, she was going to be in my life and plus I was getting humongous. I had to homeschool because I was pregnant, huge, and high risk. My fiancé called me twice a week. Then the calls stopped. *"What happened?"* I am 17 with a baby on the way and now everything he told me was a lie. Even his parents had heard from him. I began to remove him from the back of my mind. I guess I got that from my mama.

Well Dec 6, 1988, I went in at 6 am, I was in labor. *"Lord Jesus what was kicking me in my back?"* My water bag was bust at the hospital and it was show time. I swore I was never fucking again. This shit is unbearable. *"Give me a gun I am going to kill myself and get this shit over with!"* They gave me an epidural, which slowed up the labor pains yet a little too slow. Around 4 pm, it was, *"on and poppin."* The labor pains started all over again. My mama could not take the pain I was in. I was a *"size 5"* when I first got pregnant and was carrying a 10-pound baby boy. *"YES POUNDS!"* It was slow torture. Then the phone rings in my hospital room. *"Guess Who?" "My infamous baby daddy!"* By then I did not want to talk to Jesus. I could have killed a *"GROWN"* man. Then around 6:00 pm my son made his entrance into the world. I had two crying grandmothers, a crying baby daddy, two crying grandfathers and a question? *"What the hell they crying for?"* I just had a 10-pound baby who *"had split my ass wide open!"*

Finally, me and my son was home. I had a surprise visitor waiting for me. *"MY GRANDMOTHER FLEW IN ALL THE WAY FROM GARY, INDIANA!"* I had missed her so much. The first thing I remember her saying is *"Gimmie that Baby!"* Gladly! I had stitches from the *"ruddy"* to the *"tuddy!"* I am still trying to figure out who, *"ruddy,"* and *"tuddy"* is, *"Lol?"* I was in pain *"Lord Jesus."* Using my Grandmothers old remedies, Lysol and warm water to clean my stitches. I was miserable and it was not just because of my pain. My mama, my grandmother, my Fiancé's mother and my crying Baby was five minutes from putting me in a psychiatric ward! I know they all loved me and Mama was on vacation. I remembered I need her to go back to work, I needed to stop seeing my future mother in law every day and my grandmother had two more weeks in Houston. I just wanted to sleep. *"JESUS TAKE THE WHEEL,"* yet later I found out that *"JESUS didn't have no Driver's License! Lord Help!!"*

CHAPTER 13
Life Kicked In

Well, it was *"six mo"* months before I graduate from high school and my fiancé, well should I say baby's dad had fell off, *"REALLY!"* Well let that be the reason. My son was always with my mom. I swear that woman had a baby. He was her everything. I was in school getting ready for prom, cap and gown pictures and I was 17 then. I met a friend that did not go to school with me, but she taught me the ropes. Back then Deussen Park was still jumping and everybody was bumping "Too Short", then after the park, it was off to club "Gucci's." My new friend and I were fine too. She was from Clinton Park, I mean *"Beautiful."* Her mom was white and her dad was black yet I never understood her and her mom's relationship.

This girl used to literally fight her mother. She was a year younger than me, but she introduced me to the game. We partied our ass off and stayed in a dude's car with no license. That was my ride or die. We used to party and by then my son was three months and no call from baby daddy. It was cool though because I had men that was willing to step up to the plate. In school, I went to a talent show and it was a mixture of students from both district's high schools. It was on and popping. I had seen this dude across the masses of people. I asked my girl Q *"who is that?"* She said that was her daughter's father best friend Mitchell! I was in awe. Phyliss was wilding out, but my eye was on the prize and what I saw I got. I put in a word and in three weeks we were dating. *"BABY DADDY WHO?"* Yeah I was 17 about to graduate and was over that Cat. I thank my girl Q for that hookup! We rode four deep in her boyfriends truck. We ended up being the best of friends.

Well it was prom time. Me and Q had sat at *"HOUSE OF BROWN all GOT DAMN DAY!"* Shit we had a prom to go too and I still needed to glue on my nails. I was *"dooed up"* and *"spritzed up"* courtesy of my beautician Val. I got home around 7ish and my Mom had already rented my dress and of course, Mitchell was my date. My fiancé's big mouth ass sister was a substitute teacher. Oh I failed to mention that. *"I HATED THAT BITCH!" "UGH!"* Well, *"anywho,"* as I was getting ready for prom my baby daddies mom come slanging the screen door to my mama's house, *"SHE WASN'T READY!"* If she only knew she busted through the wrong *"GOT DAMN DOOR!"*

They did not get physical, but when my Mama got through chopping her ass up, not to mention that raggedy ass baby daddy I had. She left with *"NO PRIDE!" "BYE FELICIA!"* She felt I should miss my pride for her *"deadbeat"* son. Like my mama said *"BITCH PLEASE!"* Well it was 8 pm and my mama did not play. This was not even Mitchell's prom, but he was gone pay for his tux and the rental we rode in. Talking about a *"Boss!" "MY MAMA WAS A BEAST!"* He pulled up and *"DAMN HE WAS FINE!"* Of Course I was finer. We had a ball that night. Just for one thing. On my prom night, I was on my period. *"SHIT!"* We went to prom and it was *"Cinderella and Prince Charming"* stepping in that joint. Mitchell and I was sharper than a *"Mosquito's Pita Honey."* Yes even his sock's was the bomb! I had the finest man in the hotel. Me and Q ended up together that night being our boyfriends were best friends. After prom, we ended up at the Strawberry Punch Restaurant and off to Galveston we went with *"Jodeci,"* playing loudly in our rented Grand Prix life was Grand.

After prom weekend was over, that following weekend my girl Phyllis took me to a new club called the *"Benz"* on the Southside. *"FRESH MEAT! YES WE WERE WELL PAID HOES!" "WE DID NOTHING FOR FREE!"* Her and Q were my Girls. Years later, both of my girls died from *"HIV,"* unbelievable. *"Damn, rest easy to my potnas,"* I was on my on.

Well my dad still lived on Antoine and down the street was a club called *"OPP." "FRESHMEAT!"* By then me and my friend Nona was partying. Chocolate men that spoke Spanish, *"Colombians,"* is what they called. Then I met one named Cholo! He was giving me money by the shopping bags and I was running drugs all over the USA. I was his passport. I pushed a brand new big body Mercedes-Benz off the showroom floor and we lived on Houston's Southwest side. We stayed together so long I started speaking Spanish. We used to also go to this club called the Palladium and back then the club was recorded live. I had a homeboy from my neck of the woods Chi-Town 45 minutes from Gary, Indiana named DJ Lonnie Mack my boy. I put him in the game. We were tight and eventually he got tight with my people years later. One night he was coming home and dudes tried to rob him. He was shot and killed, but he did not die alone. He went out like *"John Wayne in a Western"* around this bitch. He downed one of them punk motherfuckers. *"R.I.P My Nigga a real gangsta."* Not like these *"New Breed Punk motherfuckers,"* here in Houston.

I was into all kinds of shit, but if it didn't make dollars it made no since to me and Cholo. We stayed out of Houston. We traveled a lot and knew everybody famous back then, From New York to Cali we were down. Then one summer he wanted to take me to Colombia. Here I am at 19 living the life. We had seen a million dollars by the time I turned 20, money was *"not a thang."* I ended up going to Cali and Colombia a beautiful country. The culture and the food was the bomb. I was in love with Cholo. The world was ours.

Well we are back in Houston and I get a call from my mom. She said your son's father was here. I was like *"so and what!?"* Then my mother had my son and she let me be free. She was raising him and did a *"DAMN GOOD"* job. I told my mom I would be there. I had a gangsta mind and mentality. I had some words for this deadbeat motherfucker. So we met and he attempted to hug me and I had my son on my hip but I pulled back. I was like here is your son. He was one-years old already and walking. He wanted to talk and he apologized. Being the Bitch I am, you know I said, *"FUCK YOU!"* All we have to talk about is my son. My attitude was oh so *"NOT BEAUTIFUL!"* *"How in the fuck you gone make a baby and don't call or shit and figure we got anything to discuss?"* I told him I got him. *"All you need to do is get to know your son. Yeah remember him Nigga! The one I named after you."* He replied, *"I am Sorry!"* In my mind *"Yeah You One Sorry Son of A Bitch!" Literally!!!!*

I went on with my life and *"now it is your turn to spend time with our son,"* and drove off in my Benz, *"Deuces Clown!"* I left and went back to the crib off *"Toni Tone Tony," "IT NEVER RAINS IN SOUTHERN CALIFORNIA!"* Yes looking like a boss bitch. I always watched my rearview because we had *"hella bread"* and I stayed loaded, cocked to aim and shoot any motherfucker that moved. Yes I had picked up a love for guns and was not afraid to use that bitch. That attitude was *"NOT BEAUTIFUL,"* but it was mine and I owned that motherfucker and played my role.

Well once again me and Cholo was at the airport getting ready to fly to New York. We hung out in the Bronx and would stay with his family off of east Tremont Avenue, but at night, we stayed in Manhattan only at the finest hotels. Well one night me and Cholo had business and I felt so not easy that night. I had always trusted Cholo's decisions, but that night I felt uneasy. I called my mother and checked on her and my son. I never told her my whereabouts, but for some reason that night I did. So that night me and Cholo jumped in a cab and headed to his family in the Bronx and we went to handle our business as usual. That night though I seen some new motherfuckers. I was strapped. Cholo had got to comfortable.

Things went how they were supposed to go and out of nowhere, *"BANG...BANG...BANG!"* I unstrapped myself, and did what a *"Gangsta Bitch"* would do, I start firing. I looked down and Cholo was down. *"WHAT THE FUCK?"* *"I got to get out this BITCH!"* All I could think about was my son. We were on the 3rd floor off of White Plains Rd. I shot the window out and jumped. God must have gave me wings because not only did I run from flying bullets I was able to run my ass off. Bloody and clothes tore off. I had to get it together I am in a strange place Cholo is dead and I was five minutes from downing myself.

I found a pay phone called my brother collect breathing hard and told him. I need a plane ticket one way from New York to Houston. I was lost! *"Dammit Cholo, I told you Baby, you were too comfortable."* I always had a change of clothes under my clothes. I went into a diner snatched off my wig, ripped off my t-shirt and caught a flight to Houston, but on my life I was coming back to get them motherfuckers, but in the *"NEXT BOOK!"* You *"NOT READY!"* My entire flight was fucked up, but I wanted *"blood!"* *"I WAS READY FOR WAR!"*